Fir

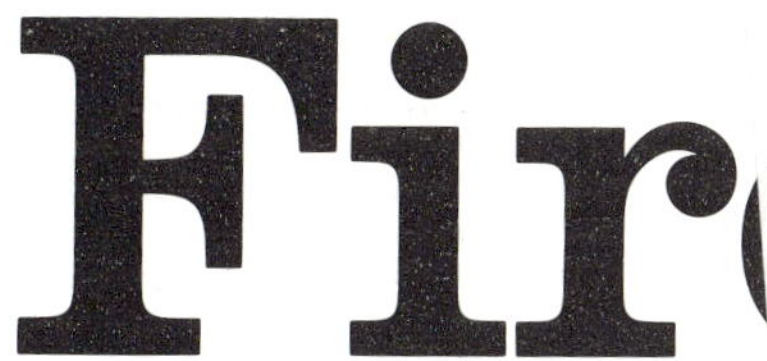

by Joan Drake

with illustrations
by Val Biro

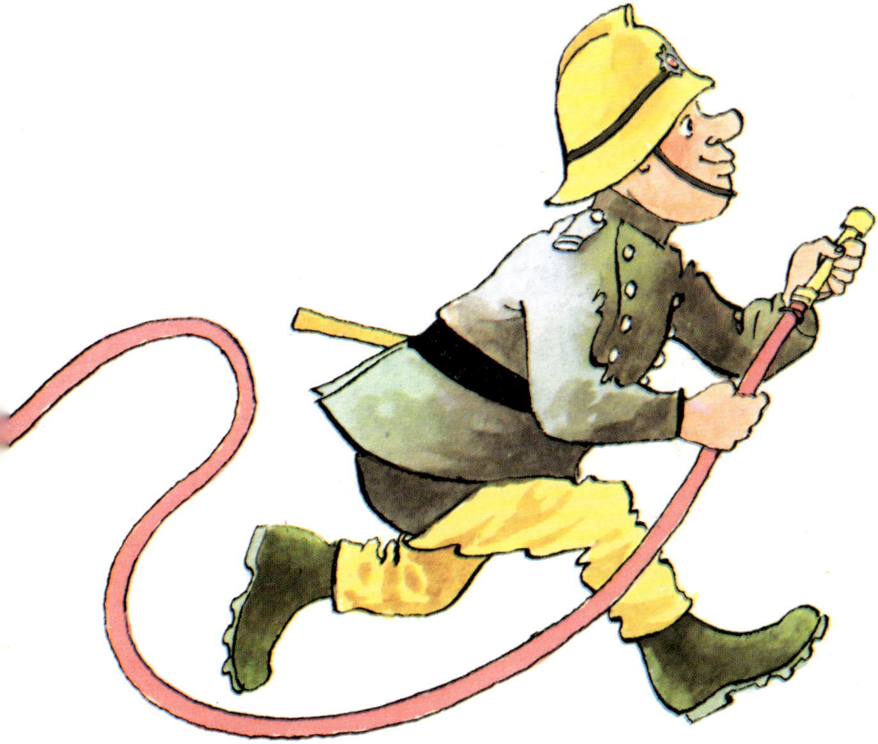

Odhams Books
London · New York · Sydney · Toronto

Peter's father went to work very early in the morning. Sometimes Peter walked with him to the bus stop.

The road was quiet. Curtains were closed and people were still asleep.

One morning, Peter saw a red glow and a curtain burning in the downstairs window of a house.

'Look, Daddy,' he pointed. 'Fire!'

71

'Quick,' said Daddy. 'Let's knock on the door. Then I'll phone the fire brigade.' Peter thumped and banged on the door.

'Fire,' he shouted. 'Get up! Fire!'

Suddenly, the quiet street was noisy with people and bells and sirens.

A police car arrived then the fire-engine dashed along.

The front door opened and through the smoke came a lady with a baby then a man carrying a little girl.

They were in night clothes.

'Please help us, ' cried the lady. 'Grandpa can't get downstairs.'

'Don't worry', said the leading fireman in big boots and helmet. 'Leave it to us.'

Firemen ran with hoses, water spraying.

Two firemen went inside and came out carrying Grandpa.

Everyone cheered. Soon the fire was out.

'Just one room damaged,' said the leading fireman, smiling at Peter. 'It was lucky this young man spotted the fire.'

'Thank you all for helping us,' said the lady. 'You saved us and our home.'

The firemen rolled up the hoses and the fire-engine left.

People walked away.

Peter's father went to work.

Peter ran home to tell his mother about his adventure.

'I'm going to be a fireman and save people when I grow up,' he said.

'Good for you,' smiled Mummy.